My Science Library

Earth's Changing Surface

by Conrad J. Storad

Science Content Editor:
Kristi Lew

Rourke
Educational Media

rourkeeducationalmedia.com

Science content editor: Kristi Lew
A former high school teacher with a background in biochemistry and more than 10 years of experience in cytogenetic laboratories, Kristi Lew specializes in taking complex scientific information and making it fun and interesting for scientists and non-scientists alike. She is the author of more than 20 science books for children and teachers.

www.rourkeeducationalmedia.com

To Jacob and Bennett. Never stop learning!
-- Grandpa Top

Photo credits: Cover © beboy, Cover logo frog © Eric Pohl, test tube © Sergey Lazarev; Page 5 © Ragnarock; Page 6 © wacpan; Page 7 © Fremme, hagit berkovich; Page 9 © Anthro; Page 10 © ollirg; Page 11 © Vulkanette; Page 12 © hagit berkovich; Page 13 © Jerry Sharp; Page 15 © Anton Petrus; Page 16/17 © Fremme; Page 19 © Angel's Gate Photography; Page 21 © Ryszard Stelmachowicz;

Editor: Kelli Hicks

Cover and page design by Nicola Stratford, bdpublishing.com

Library of Congress Cataloging-in-Publication Data

Storad, Conrad J.
 Earth's changing surface / Conrad J. Storad.
    p. cm. -- (My science library)
 Includes bibliographical references and index.
 ISBN 978-1-61741-736-8 (Hard cover) (alk. paper)
 ISBN 978-1-61741-938-6 (Soft cover)
 1. Earth--Surface--Juvenile literature. I. Title.
 QE511.S7238 2012
 551.3--dc22
                                2011003868

Printed in China, FOFO I - Production Company
 Shenzhen, Guangdong Province

Rourke Educational Media
rourkeeducationalmedia.com

customerservice@rourkeeducationalmedia.com • PO Box 643328 Vero Beach, Florida 32964

Table of Contents

Surface Features

The Earth's **surface** is made of land and water. It includes the oceans and all of the land above and below the oceans.

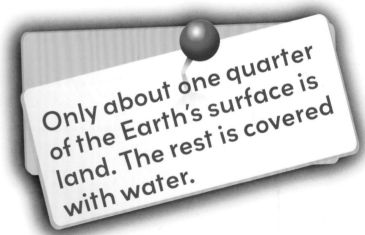

Only about one quarter of the Earth's surface is land. The rest is covered with water.

There are many bumps and grooves on Earth's surface. These bumps and grooves are called landforms.

Mountains are the tallest landform on Earth.

Fast or slow, Earth's surface is always changing.

slow change

fast change

Quick Changes

The Earth's surface is made of many big slabs. **Faults** are giant cracks between the slabs. These slabs can move and slip past each other at faults.

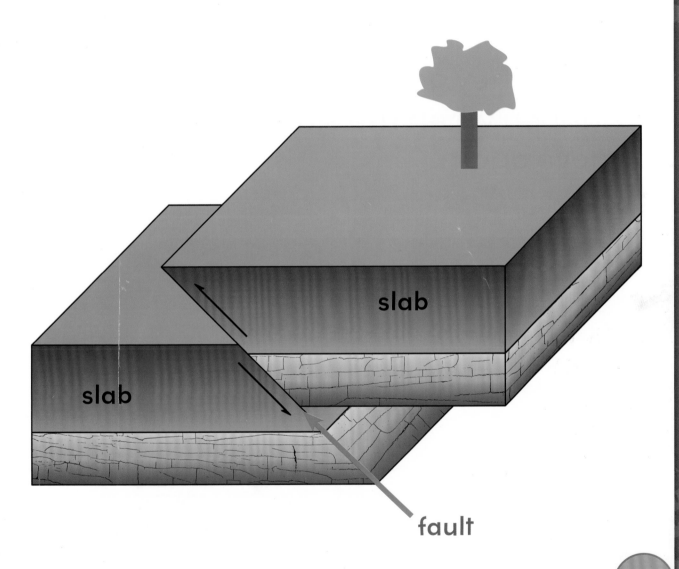

slab

slab

fault

Sometimes when the slabs move, they get stuck. **Earthquakes** happen when the slabs start to move again.

A **volcano** is an opening in the Earth's surface. Molten rock from inside can spew out in fiery explosions.

Landslides and mudslides also cause quick changes.

Floods can quickly cover areas of land with water. When the water goes away the land is changed.

Slow Changes

Not all changes happen fast. Water, ice, and wind slowly wear down rock into tiny bits. This process is called **erosion**.

Ocean waves change the shape of beaches and cliffs.

15

Over time, rivers can carve deep canyons out of solid rock.

The Grand Canyon in Arizona is almost one mile (1.61 kilometers) deep.

Strong winds move sand grain by grain. Giant piles are called dunes.

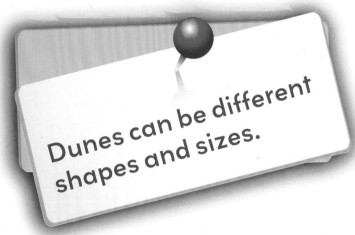

Dunes can be different shapes and sizes.

A **glacier** is a huge mass of snow and ice. It pushes tons of soil as it slowly flows over the surface.

Glaciers help to form lakes and valleys.

1. What do parts of the Earth's surface look like?

2. Name some of the things that can cause Earth's surface to change quickly.

3. Explain some of the things that change Earth's surface slowly.

Glossary

earthquakes (urth-KWAYKS): sudden, violent shaking of the Earth that may damage buildings and cause injuries

erosion (i-ROH-zhuhn): the wearing away of something by water, wind, or glacial ice

faults (FAWLTZ): large break in the Earth's surface where earthquakes can occur

glacier (GLAY-shur): a slow-moving mass of ice often found in mountain valleys or polar regions

surface (SUR-fis): the outside or outermost layer of something

volcano (vahl-KAY-noh): an opening in the Earth's surface through which molten lava, ash, and hot gases erupt, sometimes violently

Index

Websites

www.extremescience.com

www.geography4kids.com

www.kidsgeo.com

www.fema.gov/kids/volcano.htm

About the Author

Conrad J. Storad is the award-winning author of more than 30 books for young readers. He writes about desert animals, plants, creepy crawlers, and planets. Conrad lives in Tempe, Arizona with his wife Laurie and their little double dapple wiener dog, Sophia. They love to explore Arizona's deserts and mountains.

Photo by Tom Story